Things to

gliders, propellers, hang glider-kite and others

A Puffin Book
Written, illustrated and produced by Jack Newnham
Copyright © Penguin Books Australia Ltd, 1980

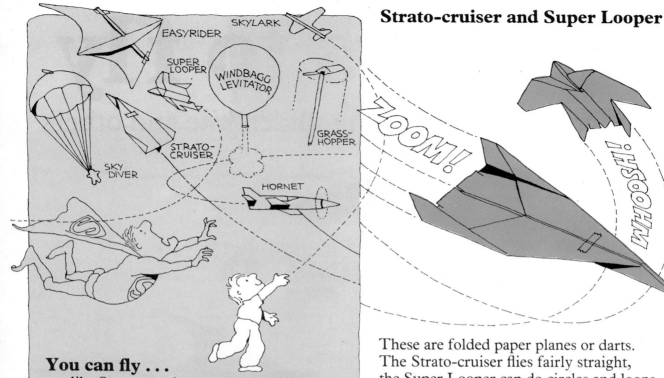

Strato-cruiser and Super Looper

You can fly ...

not like Superman, but you can **make** things that fly. That's where the fun is – making them and getting them to fly.

Here are 8 different flying things – mostly made of paper, card and sticky tape.

There are 2 folded darts that stunt; an outdoor glider that can fly so high it might get lost; a hang glider that you tow up on a line and then let go; a sort of helicopter thing; a 'buzz' plane with a spinning propeller; a jet propelled balloon and a parachute. The hang glider is also a kite.

Don't think that because they are only made of paper they won't fly well – start making them and find out for yourself.

These are folded paper planes or darts. The Strato-cruiser flies fairly straight, the Super Looper can do circles and loops.

Get some sheets of writing paper – the stiffer kind (bond), not thin (bank). You may have to cut them to get the right size. Notice that the Looper sheet is cut narrower.

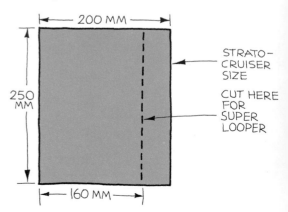

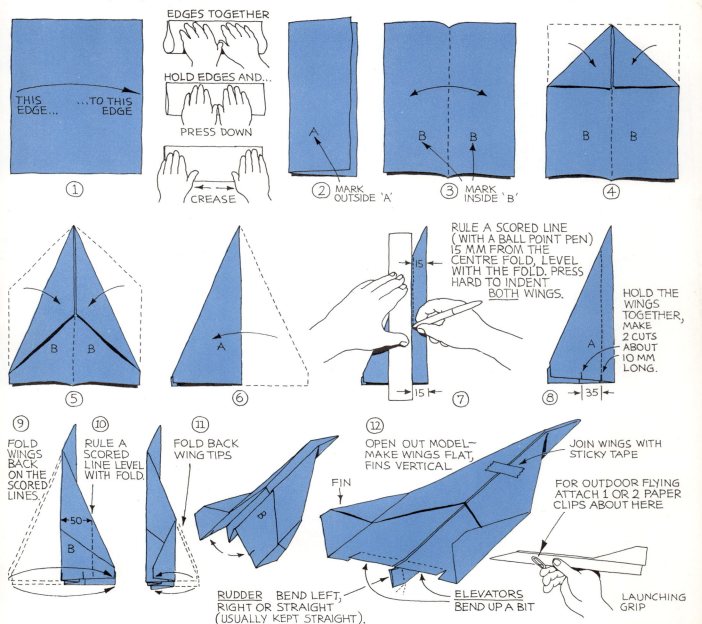

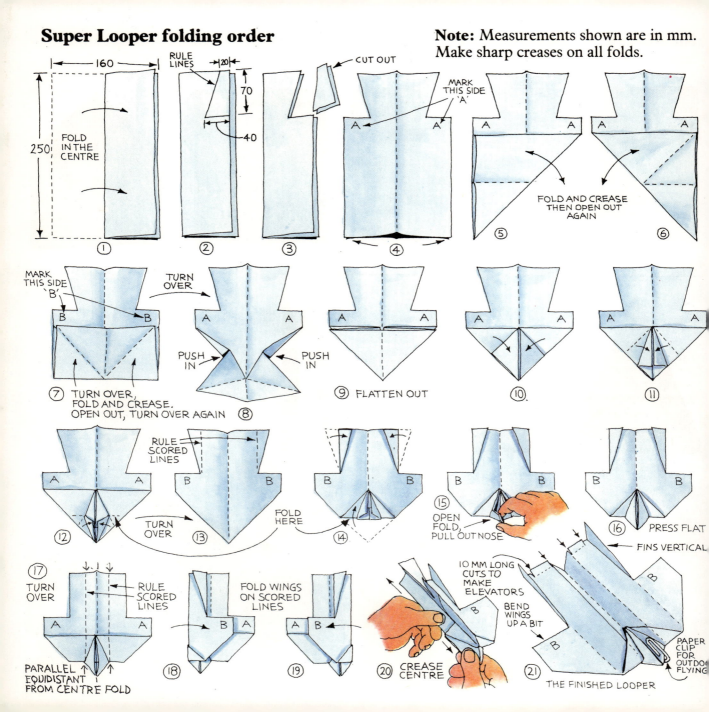

Flying paper planes

You can fly indoors – or outside on calm days. Don't let them get wet. Don't worry if your first flights are not so good – there are things you can do to make them fly better.

Elevators: Bending these up brings the nose up – bending them down makes it dive.

Rudder: Bending the rudder left (looking from the back), makes the plane turn left. Bend it right for a right turn. On the Looper you can bend both rudders.

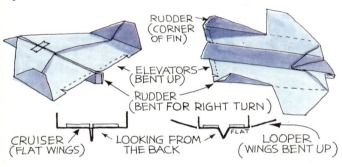

RUDDER (CORNER OF FIN)
ELEVATORS (BENT UP)
RUDDER (BENT FOR RIGHT TURN)
CRUISER (FLAT WINGS) — LOOKING FROM THE BACK — FLAT — LOOPER (WINGS BENT UP)

Launching: Launch with a fairly hard throw. Aim low to skim the ground, or high for longer flights. Launching with banked wings (one wing low), makes the model turn – even with a straight rudder.

Try to get your Cruiser to make a wide, graceful circle back to your hand. Use plenty of 'up' elevator, but <u>not much</u> rudder. Launch <u>fast</u>, aim straight ahead, with wings <u>banked</u> to help it turn.

LEFT WING LOW (BANKED LEFT)
BEND RUDDER LEFT A LITTLE OR STRAIGHT

Aerobatics for Super Looper

With practice you should be able to do these and other stunts you make up yourself. The trick is to get the right elevator and rudder setting with the right launching angle.

Loops: Bend elevators <u>up</u>, rudders <u>straight</u>, wings <u>level</u>. If it turns left or right, correct by turning the rudders in the opposite direction.

MODEL GOING INTO LOOP AFTER MAKING AN 'S' TURN

Circles: For tight circles to right, bend rudders <u>right</u>, elevators <u>up</u>. Launch with wings banked <u>right</u>. For wide circles – elevators <u>flat</u>.

'S' turns: Bend rudders <u>left</u>, wings banked <u>right</u>.

BANKED RIGHT

Outside loop and catch: Bend elevators <u>down</u>, rudders <u>straight</u>, wings <u>level</u>.

Skylark – an outdoor 'chuck' glider

Here is a model for flying outside on fine days. It flies better than a folded plane because it has a better shape – more like a real plane. It is made of stiffer paper. The wings are not flat. They are 'dished' underneath and 'humped' on top. This is called 'cambering'. A bird's wing is shaped like this. It gives more 'lift' than a flat wing. If your Skylark gets into rising air it could go very high and travel a long way.

You will need a sheet of stiff drawing paper (cartridge paper), some thin card, a piece of plasticine, a paper clip and some sticky tape.

About the pattern: Like other models in this book, you need to copy the printed pattern to get the right shape. The best way to do this is to prick the dots (marked with numbers) through the page onto your paper or card placed underneath. By ruling lines joining the pinholes you copy the pattern. If you don't want to make holes in the page, trace the pattern onto tracing paper and prick through the tracing. If you want to make lots of models, make cardboard templates.

Preparing the paper: Cut a rectangle of drawing paper to the size shown. Rule the scored line. Scoring makes it easy to fold. Use a ball point pen. An old dried up pen is best if you don't want an ink line showing. Press down hard with the pen so that it makes an indentation along the line. Fold the paper. Hold the sheets together with a piece of tape.

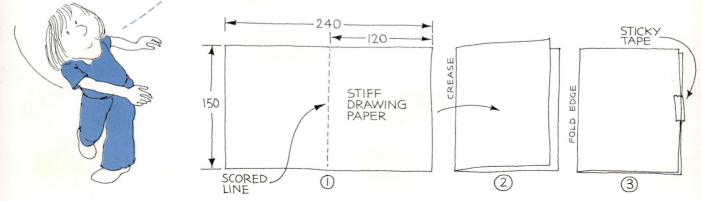

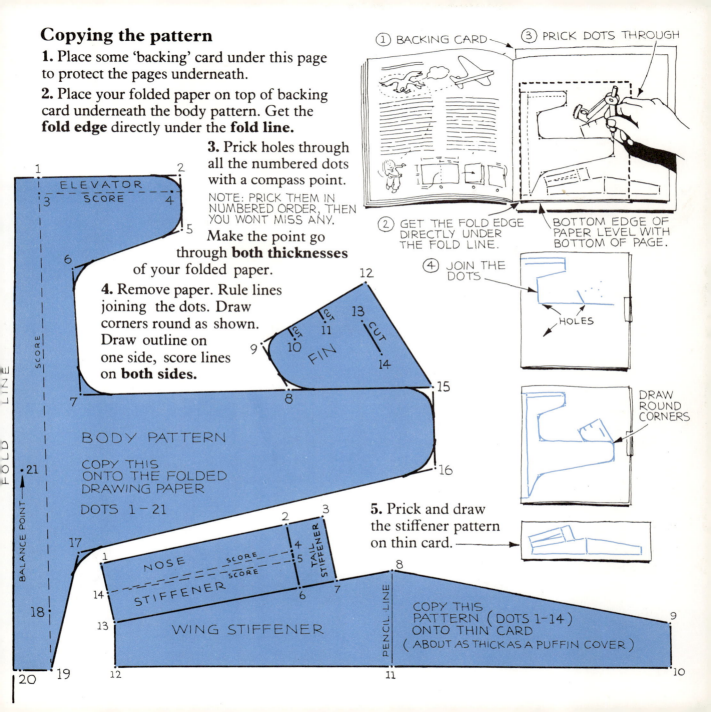

Cutting and assembling Skylark

Cut out the parts with scissors. The tape holds the sheets together while you cut the body pattern, so cut the wing tips last.

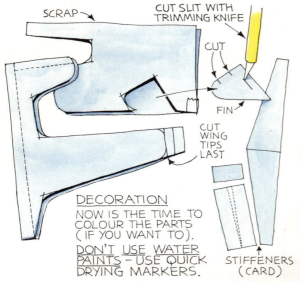
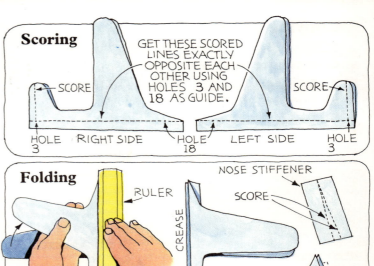
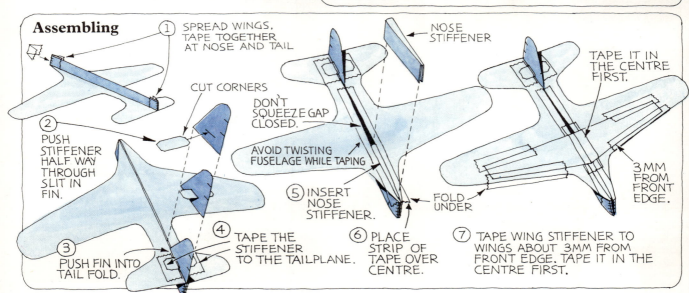

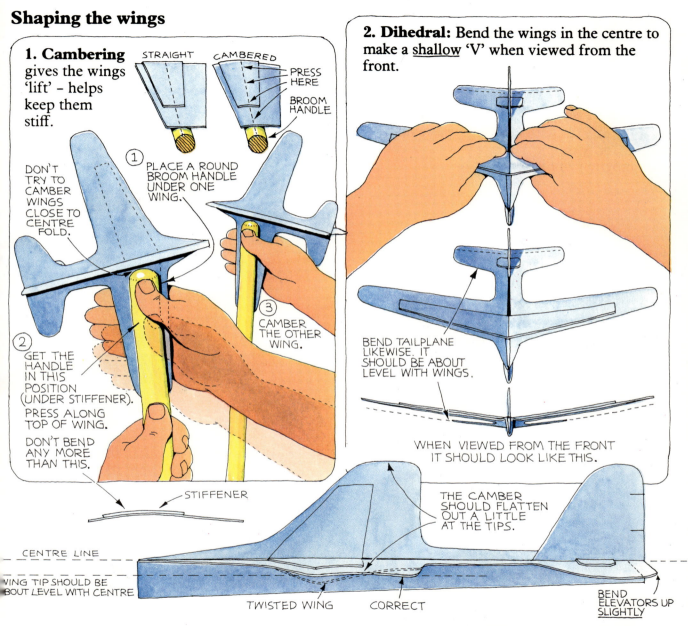

Getting it ready to fly

Waterproofing: In damp or humid air paper planes fly like banana skins — sloppy, because the paper becomes soft. They must stay stiff if they are to fly well.

Wiping all over with floor wax (paste not liquid), or 'Vaseline' helps to protect them. Aluminium paint is good but heavier.

WIPE ALL OVER WITH WAX. DO EACH PART IN TURN — FLAT, ON A TABLE EDGE. WHEN FINISHED, CHECK SHAPE OF WINGS AND TAIL. RE-CAMBER THE WINGS IF NECESSARY.

Balance: The model should balance horizontally when suspended from the balance point (hole 21).

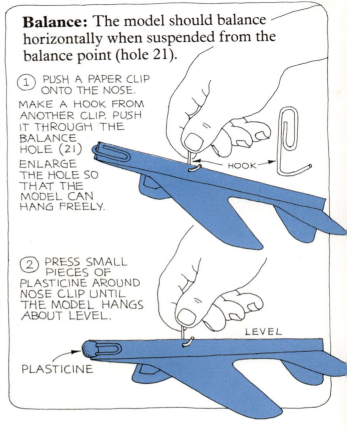

① PUSH A PAPER CLIP ONTO THE NOSE. MAKE A HOOK FROM ANOTHER CLIP. PUSH IT THROUGH THE BALANCE HOLE (21) ENLARGE THE HOLE SO THAT THE MODEL CAN HANG FREELY.

② PRESS SMALL PIECES OF PLASTICINE AROUND NOSE CLIP UNTIL THE MODEL HANGS ABOUT LEVEL.

Control surfaces: These parts affect flight performance. Straighten them if they get bent.

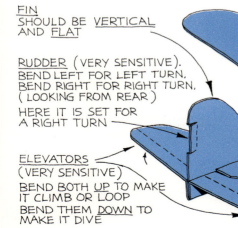

FIN SHOULD BE VERTICAL AND FLAT

RUDDER (VERY SENSITIVE). BEND LEFT FOR LEFT TURN, BEND RIGHT FOR RIGHT TURN, (LOOKING FROM REAR) HERE IT IS SET FOR A RIGHT TURN

ELEVATORS (VERY SENSITIVE) BEND BOTH UP TO MAKE IT CLIMB OR LOOP BEND THEM DOWN TO MAKE IT DIVE

TAILPLANE SHOULD BE FLAT — SAME DIHEDRAL AS WINGS.

WINGS SHOULD BE STRAIGHT — NO TWISTS.

FOR LONG, HIGH FLIGHTS LIKE THIS YOU NEED TO GET THE ELEVATORS AND RUDDER SET JUST RIGHT. YOU ALSO NEED A GOOD HARD THROW. IN A BREEZE, IT MAY NEED A LITTLE MORE NOSE-WEIGHT.

Flying the Skylark

Where and when to fly: The Skylark is meant for flying outside. You can fly on calm or breezy days. You will need lots of space.

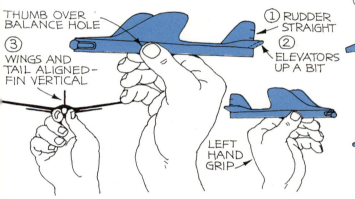

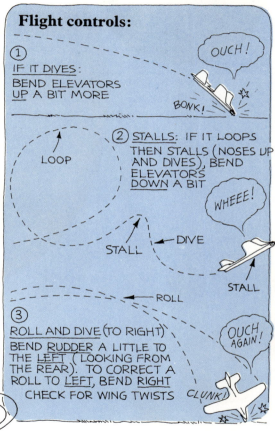

Flight controls:

① IF IT DIVES: BEND ELEVATORS UP A BIT MORE

② STALLS: IF IT LOOPS THEN STALLS (NOSES UP AND DIVES), BEND ELEVATORS DOWN A BIT

③ ROLL AND DIVE (TO RIGHT) BEND RUDDER A LITTLE TO THE LEFT (LOOKING FROM THE REAR). TO CORRECT A ROLL TO LEFT, BEND RIGHT CHECK FOR WING TWISTS

Launching: 1. Bend elevators up a bit. 2. Rudder straight. 3. Wings and tail aligned, fin vertical (see drawing).

Hold it as shown. Launch it fast and high straight into the wind.

If, after a few launches, you find it always – 1. Dives 2. Stalls or 3. Rolls, adjust the controls as shown. Try to get it to climb steeply, then fly in wide circles coming down to land.

You will get good long flights when you get the elevators just right – a sort of balance between stalling and diving. Set the rudder to give **wide** circles – it may circle naturally with straight rudder.

Get to know your model. Keep making small adjustments to elevators and rudder to make it do things. In a breeze, Skylark may go high and far. Don't worry if you lose it, you can soon make another.

LAUNCH FAST INTO THE WIND (IF ANY)

Making the tubes

There is an outside tube (made of drawing paper), and an inside tube (made of plastic because it gets wet when you blow).

The outer tube

Drawing paper

① CUT A STRIP 80 MM LONG, 50 MM WIDE. CUT OFF THE CORNERS.

② ROLL IT TIGHTLY ONTO A ROUND PENCIL.

③ REMOVE THE PENCIL, DON'T LET THE TUBE UNROLL.

④ HOLD A RULER ACROSS ONE END, LET IT UNROLL SLOWLY UNTIL IT IS ABOUT 12 MM ACROSS INSIDE DIAMETER.

⑤ FINISH WITH 2 OR 3 TURNS OF TAPE.

FINISHED TUBE

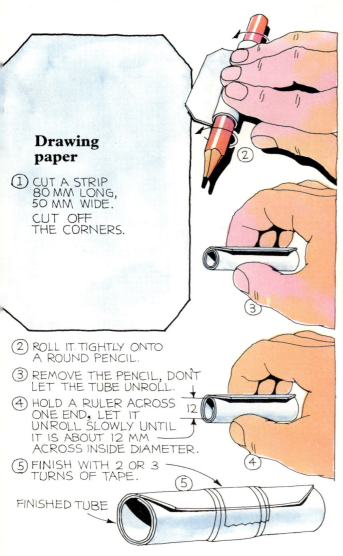

The inner tube

Don't use paper - it gets soggy. You can get plastic from a shirt box top or cosmetic pack, a margarine or 'take away' food container, or a disposable plastic cup etc. It should be soft enough for rolling tightly.

Plastic film

① CUT A STRIP 80 MM LONG, 40 MM WIDE. CUT OFF THE CORNERS.

ROLL IT AROUND A PENCIL FIRST, THIS MAY HELP YOU START THE TIGHT ROLL.

② NOW ROLL IT TIGHTLY AS SHOWN.

③ LET IT UNROLL UNTIL THE INSIDE DIAMETER IS 7·5 MM.

④ FINISH THE TUBE WITH 2 OR 3 TURNS OF TAPE.

FINISHED TUBE

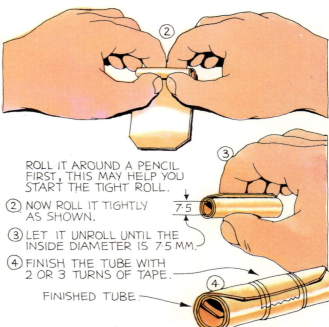

Assembling the Levitator

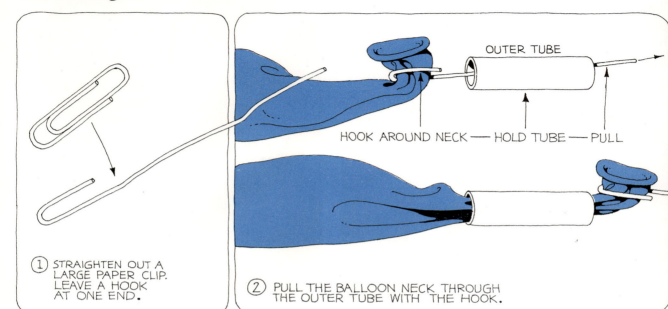

① STRAIGHTEN OUT A LARGE PAPER CLIP. LEAVE A HOOK AT ONE END.

② PULL THE BALLOON NECK THROUGH THE OUTER TUBE WITH THE HOOK.

HOOK AROUND NECK — HOLD TUBE — PULL

OUTER TUBE

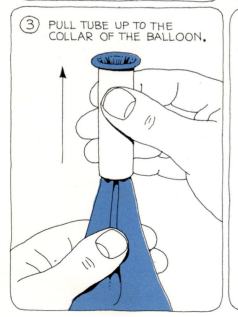

③ PULL TUBE UP TO THE COLLAR OF THE BALLOON.

④ THE INNER TUBE SHOULD FIT FAIRLY TIGHTLY INSIDE THE NECK OF THE BALLOON.

BUILD UP THE THICKNESS AROUND THE CENTRE WITH A FEW TURNS OF STICKY TAPE TO MAKE IT TIGHT.

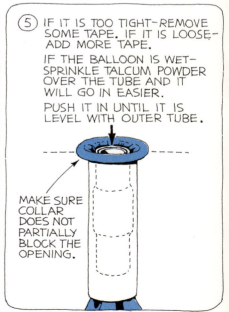

⑤ IF IT IS TOO TIGHT—REMOVE SOME TAPE. IF IT IS LOOSE—ADD MORE TAPE.

IF THE BALLOON IS WET—SPRINKLE TALCUM POWDER OVER THE TUBE AND IT WILL GO IN EASIER.

PUSH IT IN UNTIL IT IS LEVEL WITH OUTER TUBE.

MAKE SURE COLLAR DOES NOT PARTIALLY BLOCK THE OPENING.

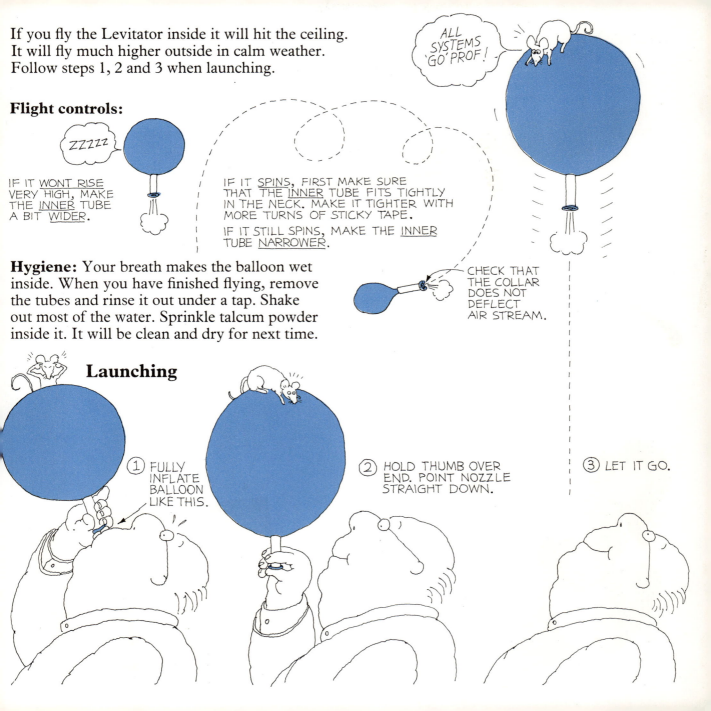

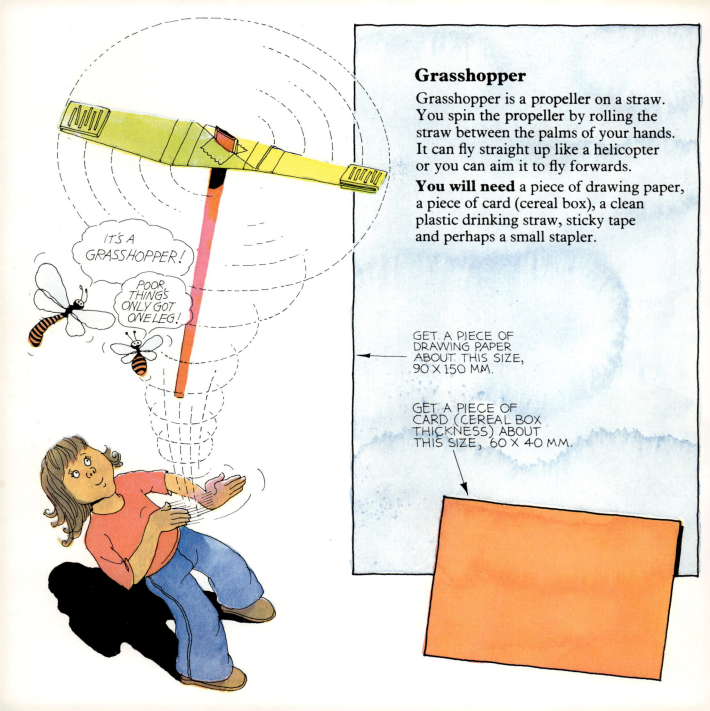

Grasshopper

Grasshopper is a propeller on a straw. You spin the propeller by rolling the straw between the palms of your hands. It can fly straight up like a helicopter or you can aim it to fly forwards.

You will need a piece of drawing paper, a piece of card (cereal box), a clean plastic drinking straw, sticky tape and perhaps a small stapler.

GET A PIECE OF DRAWING PAPER ABOUT THIS SIZE, 90 X 150 MM.

GET A PIECE OF CARD (CEREAL BOX THICKNESS) ABOUT THIS SIZE, 60 X 40 MM.

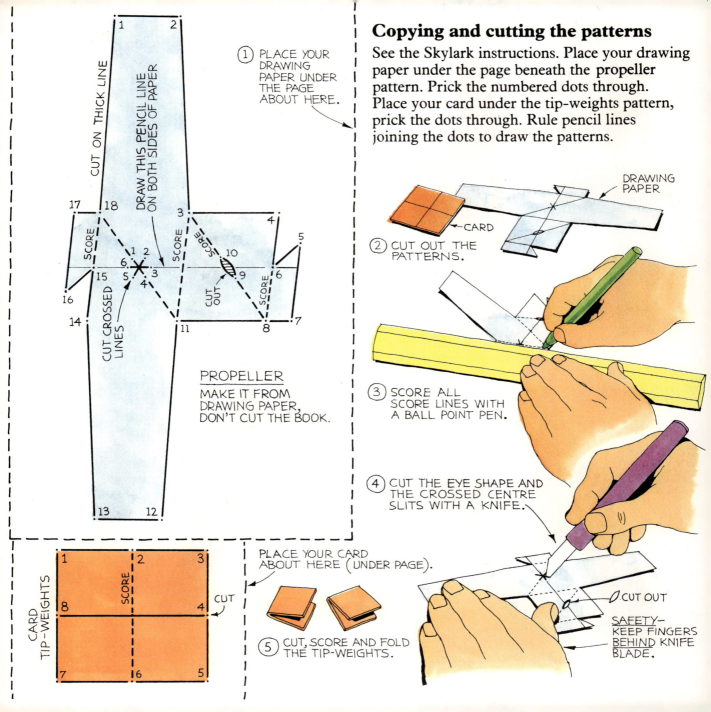

Folding and mounting the propeller

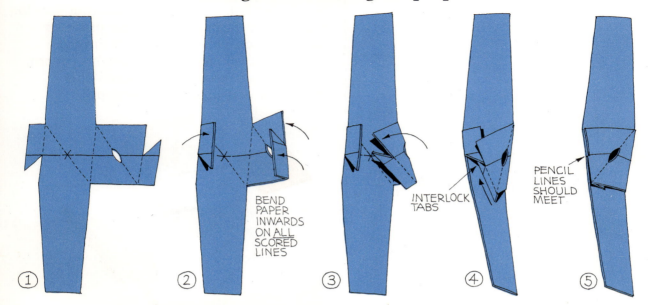

Fold the propeller as shown to get used to it – then open it out again.

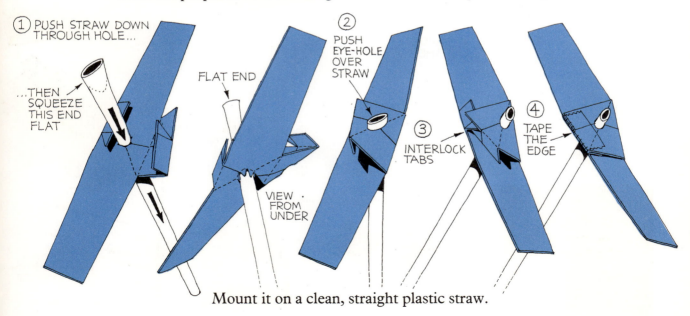

Mount it on a clean, straight plastic straw.

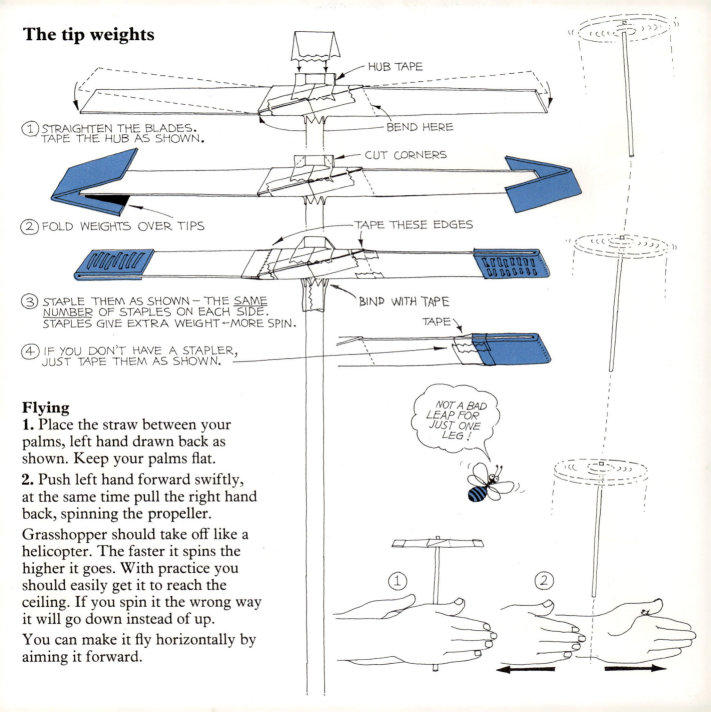

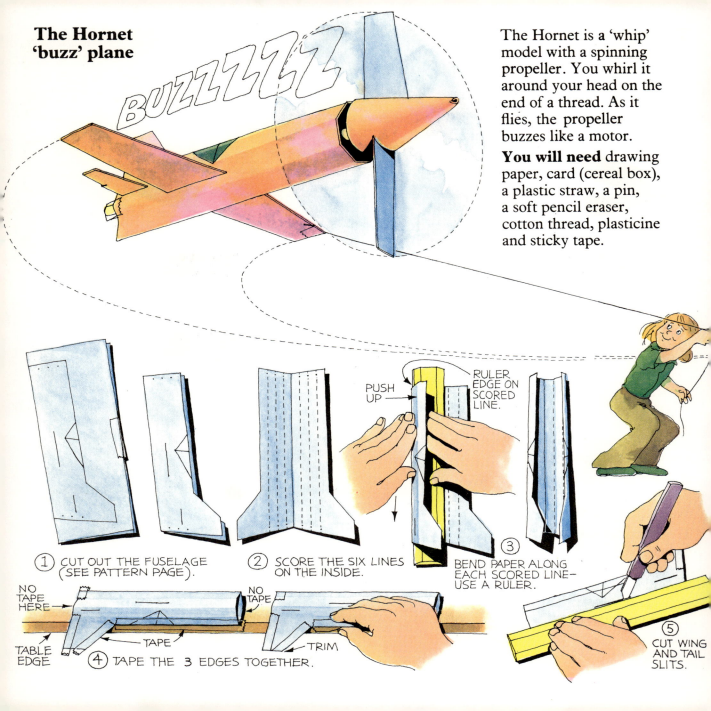

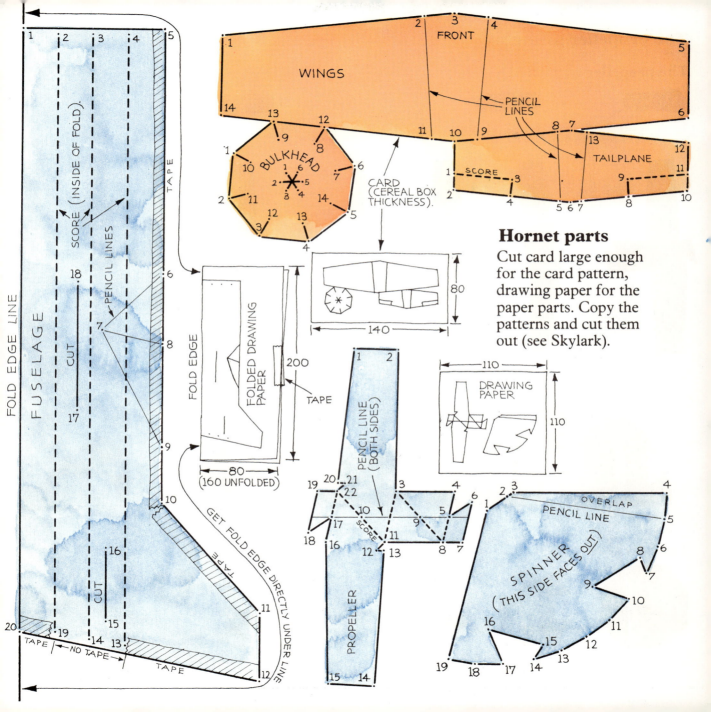

Hornet parts

Cut card large enough for the card pattern, drawing paper for the paper parts. Copy the patterns and cut them out (see Skylark).

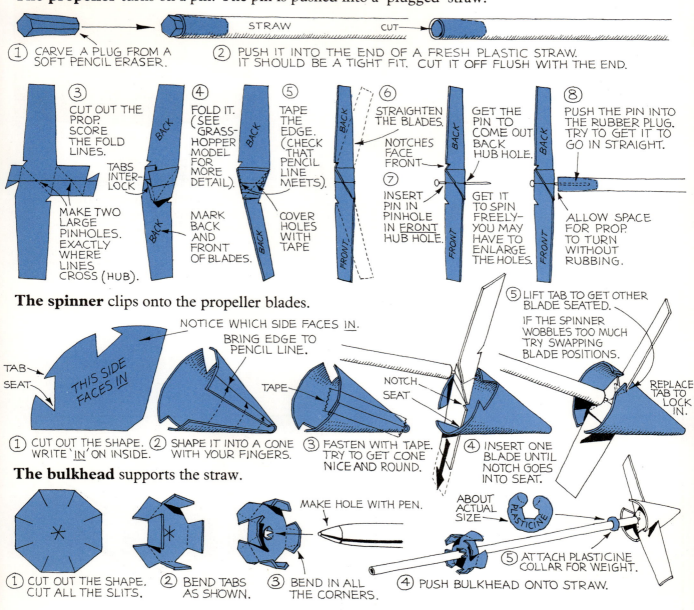

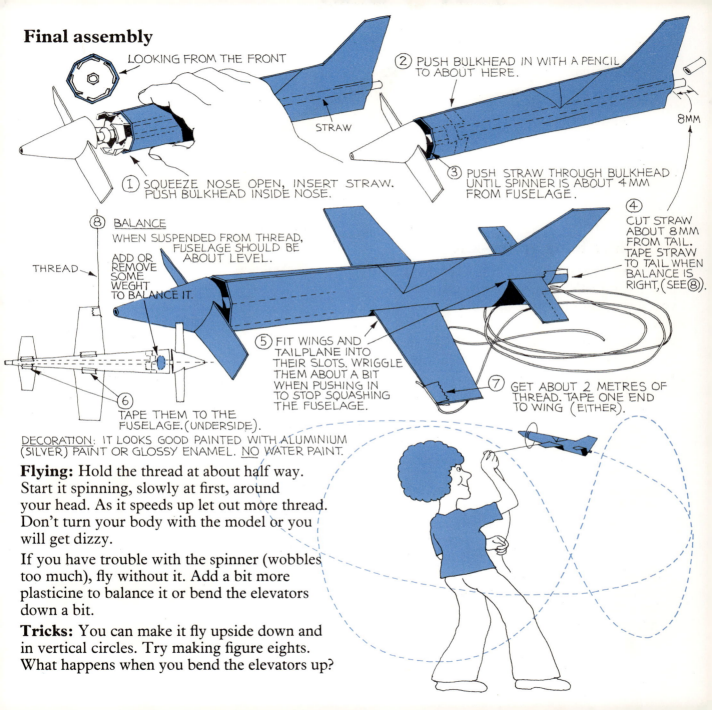

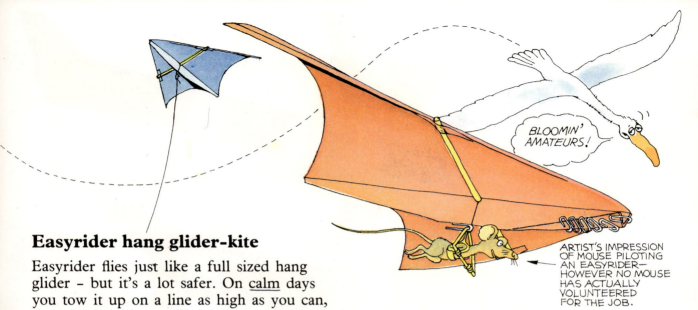

BLOOMIN' AMATEURS!

ARTIST'S IMPRESSION OF MOUSE PILOTING AN EASYRIDER– HOWEVER NO MOUSE HAS ACTUALLY VOLUNTEERED FOR THE JOB.

Easyrider hang glider-kite

Easyrider flies just like a full sized hang glider – but it's a lot safer. On <u>calm</u> days you tow it up on a line as high as you can, then the line drops off. Away she goes as free as a bird, gliding gently back to earth.

On breezy days you can fly it as a kite. Just tape the line so that it won't come off, and remove the nose weight. Hang gliders are efficient kites. When you get it flying well, it will soar directly over your head.

You will need stiff wrapping paper (brown or coloured). Newspaper is too soft. You also need a springy stick, paper clips, straws, card (cereal box), 50-100 metres of light string or strong thread and some sticky tape.

The Paper: It is important to use stiff paper because the wings must stay arched when the model is gliding. If they sag it will go into a spin and crash. Paper from a large supermarket bag is about right (although it is better to use uncreased paper), or any paper of about the same stiffness. As with the Skylark glider, waxing with floor wax helps preserve it and keep the wings stiff, but is not necessary in dry weather.

NOTE: STICKY TAPE WON'T STICK TO WAXED PAPER SO DON'T WAX IT UNTIL IT IS FINISHED.

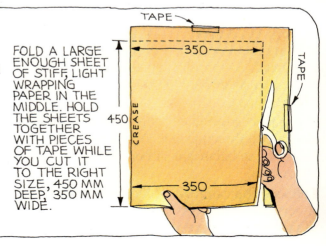

FOLD A LARGE ENOUGH SHEET OF STIFF, LIGHT WRAPPING PAPER IN THE MIDDLE. HOLD THE SHEETS TOGETHER WITH PIECES OF TAPE WHILE YOU CUT IT TO THE RIGHT SIZE, 450 MM DEEP, 350 MM WIDE.

Folding the wings

① FOLD UP CORNER FLAP. CREASE. DRAW A LINE 'A' ALONG THE TOP EDGE.

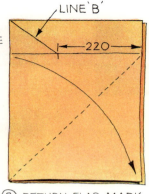
② RETURN FLAP. MARK 220MM FROM EDGE. DRAW LINE 'B'.

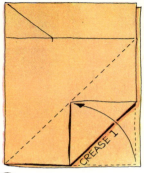
③ BRING CORNER TO CREASE-LINE. CREASE AGAIN.

THE LEADING EDGES OF THE WINGS ARE MADE STIFF BY DOUBLING THE PAPER FIVE TIMES.

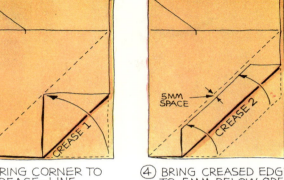
④ BRING CREASED EDGE TO 5MM BELOW CREASE-LINE. CREASE AGAIN.

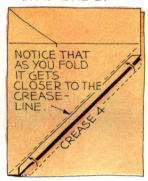
⑤ DOUBLE AND CREASE AGAIN.

⑥ DOUBLE AND CREASE AGAIN.

⑦ DOUBLE FOR THE LAST TIME. CREASE HARD.

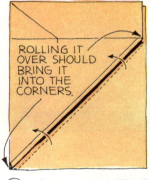
⑧ NOW <u>ROLL</u> IT OVER <u>ONCE</u>. PRESS AND HOLD.

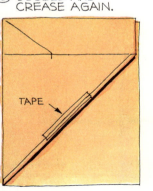
⑨ TAPE IT IN THE MIDDLE TO HOLD IT.

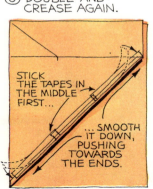
⑩ THEN TAPE THE ENDS, ONE AT A TIME.

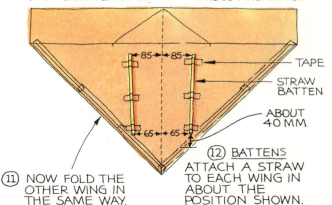
⑪ NOW FOLD THE OTHER WING IN THE SAME WAY.

⑫ <u>BATTENS</u> ATTACH A STRAW TO EACH WING IN ABOUT THE POSITION SHOWN.

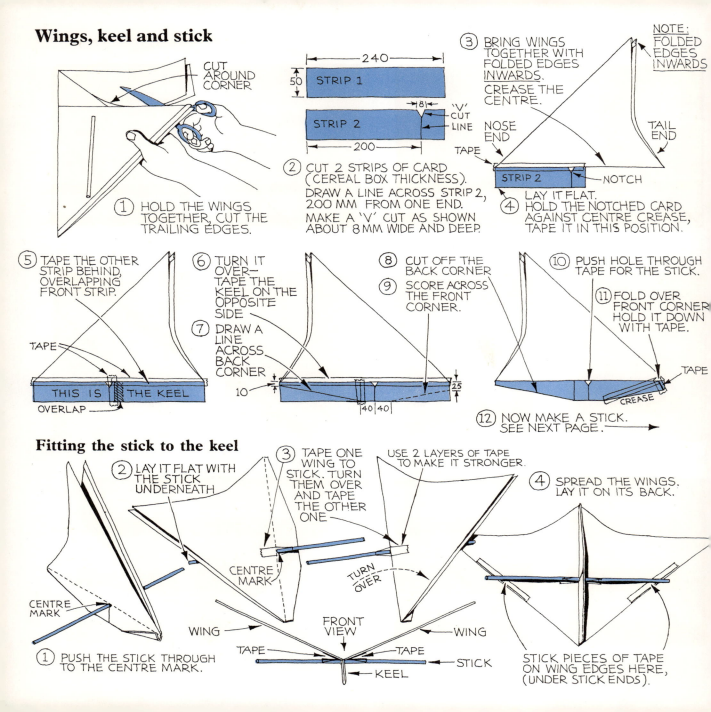

The stick

You need a light but strong 'springy' stick. Use split bamboo or a straight twig from a tree. Trim it with your knife so that it bends evenly as shown. If you can't get a wooden stick, make one out of plastic straws as shown below, but a wooden stick is best.

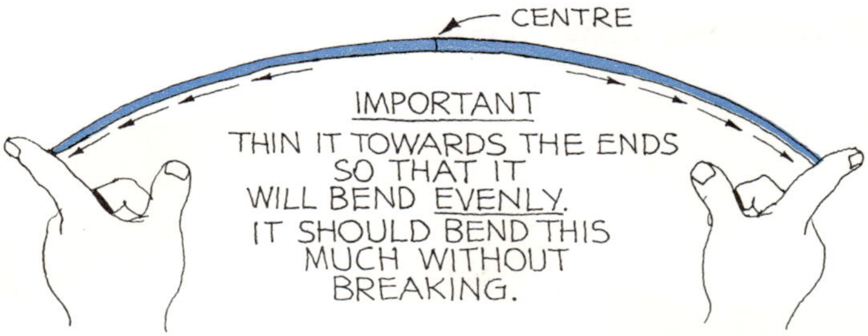

CENTRE

IMPORTANT THIN IT TOWARDS THE ENDS SO THAT IT WILL BEND <u>EVENLY</u>. IT SHOULD BEND THIS MUCH WITHOUT BREAKING.

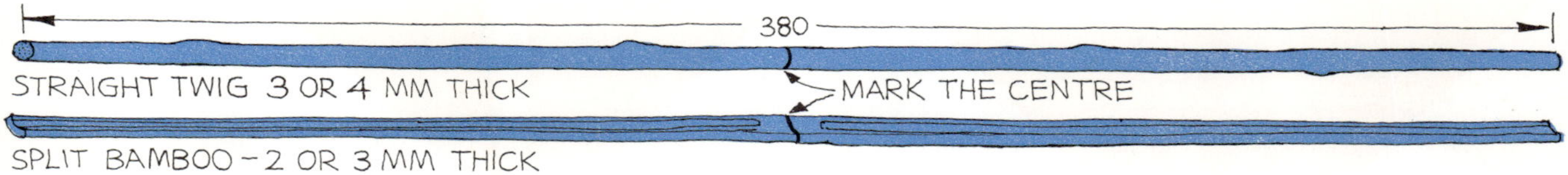

380 — MARK THE CENTRE

STRAIGHT TWIG 3 OR 4 MM THICK

SPLIT BAMBOO – 2 OR 3 MM THICK

A plastic straw stick is good for gliding. For kite flying, strengthen it with a splint, (see flying instructions). Get 8 fresh straws.

① SPLIT 6 STRAWS DOWN ONE SIDE WITH SCISSORS. IF THEY ARE SHARP YOU WON'T HAVE TO SNIP—JUST PUSH.

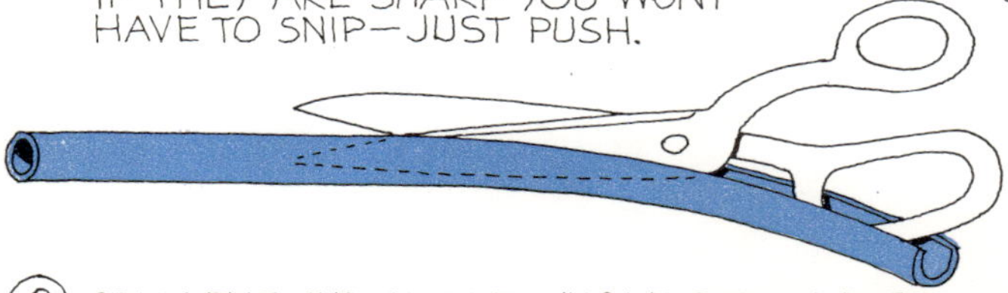

⑤ BINDING THE STRAWS
HOLD STRAW AT ABOUT THIS ANGLE. LET TAPE HANG VERTICALLY WHILE YOU ROLL THE STICK BETWEEN YOUR FINGERS. THE BINDING TAPE SHOULD OVERLAP.

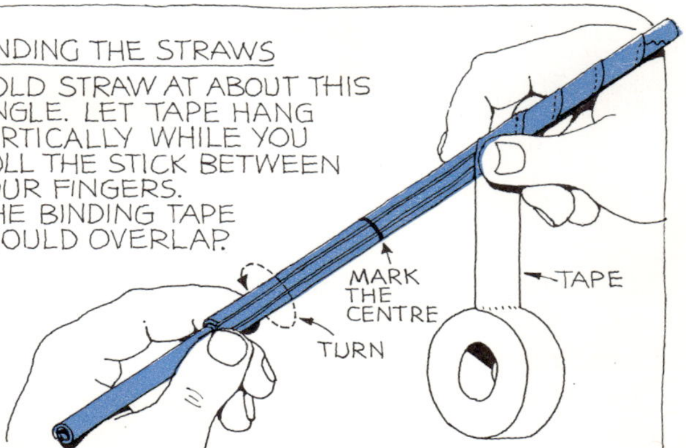

MARK THE CENTRE — TURN — TAPE

② SPLIT THE END OF ONE WHOLE STRAW. PUSH IT INTO THE END OF ANOTHER TO JOIN THEM.
BIND THE JOIN WITH ONE TURN OF TAPE

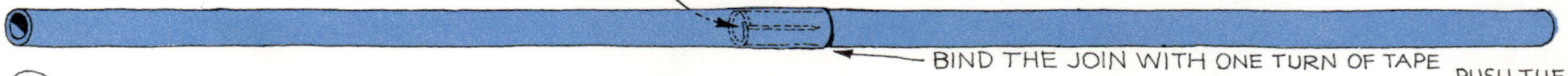

③ PUSH 2 SPLIT STRAWS OVER THE JOINED STRAWS. OVERLAP THEM IN THE CENTRE. PUSH THEM ON FROM THE ENDS

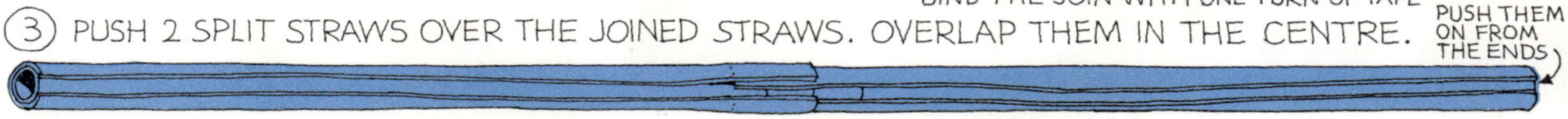

④ BUILD UP THE THICKNESS WITH 2 MORE STRAWS AND ANOTHER **TWO STRAWS** IN THE MIDDLE.
TRY TO GET THE SPLITS ON OPPOSITE SIDES.

⑤ BIND IT WITH STICKY TAPE AS SHOWN ABOVE. OVERLAP THE TURNS — IT DOESN'T MATTER IF TAPE GETS WRINKLED.

NOTE: STRAWS ARE DRAWN THICK TO MAKE THE INSTRUCTIONS CLEAR.

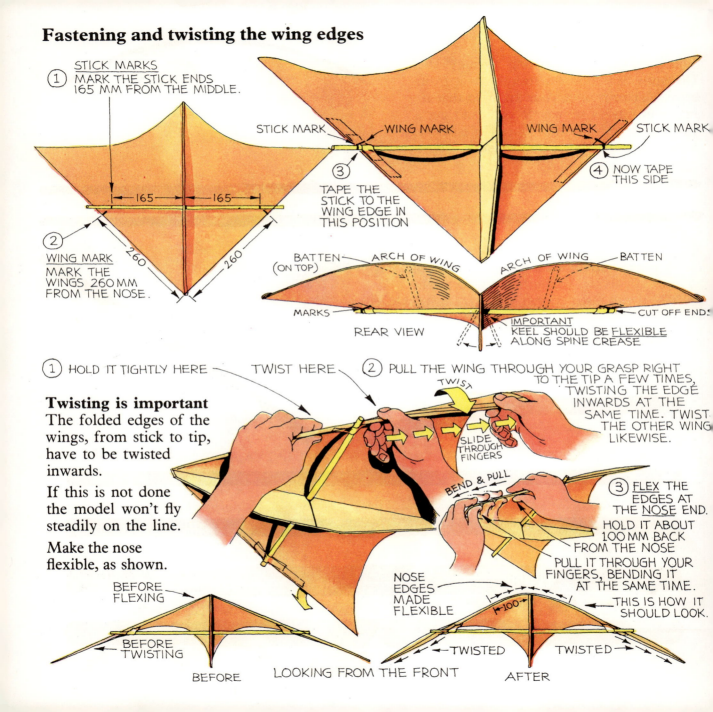

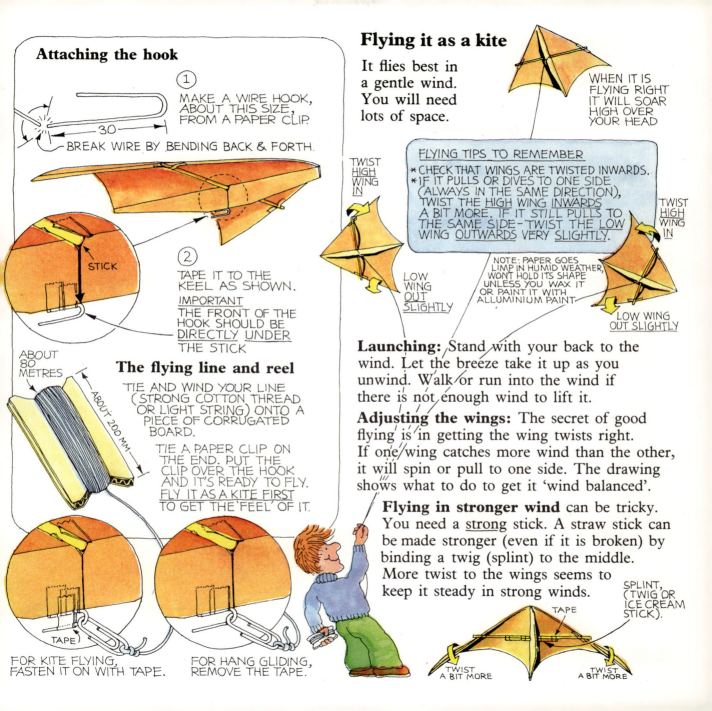

Flying it as a hang glider

As a hang glider, Easyrider is towed up high on the line, then released to glide gently back to earth.

First remove the tape 'stopper' from the hook, allowing the line to fall off. Now you get it to glide.

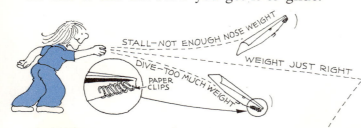

Test gliding: You will need to add weight (paper clips) to the nose. Without nose weight (ballast) it just stalls and dives. Keep adding paper clips until you get a long, flat glide. You can test glide it indoors.

Hang gliding: Take it out gliding in <u>calm</u> weather. Unlike kite flying, you don't need wind. For the first attempts use a short tow line (about 10 paces long).

Ground launch

1. With the line on the hook, put the model on the ground, nose facing into the wind (if any).

2. Stretch the line out straight ahead of it. Hold the reel and carefully take up the slack. Give a fairly sharp tug on the line to get the nose up. Keep pulling. Don't let the line go slack or it will fall off the hook. Run or walk into the wind to keep it flying.

Flight corrections: Hooray if it goes straight up. But it may pull away to one side, not getting very high. Correct it by twisting the high-wing edge in a bit. See kite flying page for more details.

Releasing: The line will fall off when you stop pulling. Don't jerk the line. Just let it fall smoothly. Easyrider should glide down slowly and land gently.

When you get it flying straight up on a short line, launch it with a longer line for really high flights.

STORAGE: TO PRESERVE THE SHAPE, HANG IT UP FROM ITS HOOK, OR UNFASTEN THE STICK AND LAY IT FLAT.

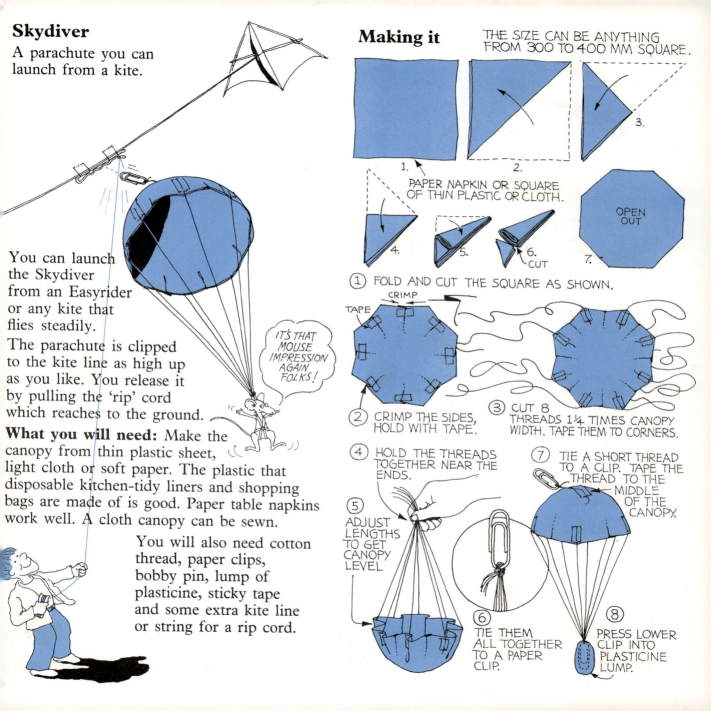

Launching Skydiver from a kite

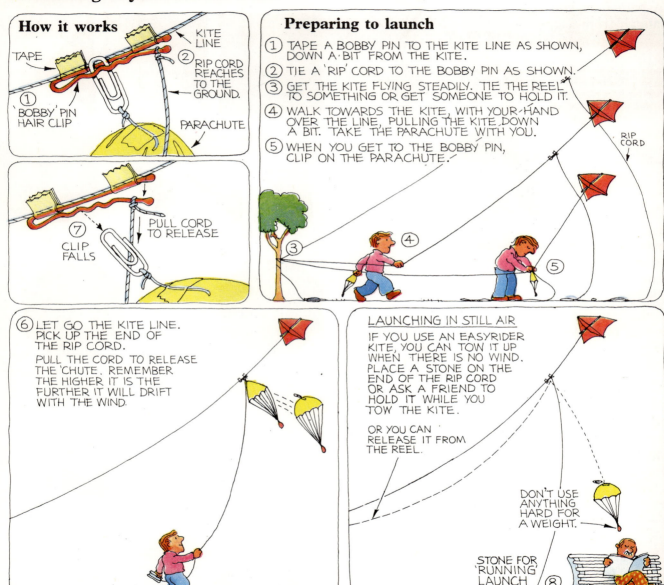

Show your friends how to make these flying things. Make some colourful ones for presents.